The Shooting Gallery
Carrie Etter

VERVE
POETRY PRESS
BIRMINGHAM

PUBLISHED BY VERVE POETRY PRESS
https://vervepoetrypress.com
mail@vervepoetrypress.com

The right of Carrie Etter to be identified as author of this work has been asserted in accordance with section 77 of the Copyright, Designs and Patents Act 1988.

FIRST PUBLISHED OCT 2020

Printed and bound in the UK
by Positive Print, Birmingham

ISBN: 978-1-912565-45-0

Cover Illustration by Linda Black

CONTENTS

Foreword

I.   Toyen, 1939-40   9

II.   The United States, 1999-   23

Acknowledgments

for Naomi Mandel

FOREWORD

In March 2019, on a visit to Prague, I encountered the work of Czech surrealist transgender artist Toyen at the Kampa Museum and the National Gallery and became deeply interested in the artist and his work. On my return to England, I began researching Toyen and occasionally composing poems in response to various paintings.

Some months later, I discovered Toyen's series of twelve line drawings, *The Shooting Gallery* (1939-40), and was intrigued by the way they combined images of war and images of childhood, as suggested by the ambiguous title: is this a shooting gallery for military training or an amusement at a fairground? I began drafting pieces in response to Toyen's drawings, imagining the prose poems as surrealist paintings in words. After I had drafted a dozen or so poems, I realised—abruptly, uneasily—I associated the combination of youth and violence with U.S. school and university shootings.

With that thought in mind, I began researching some of these shootings, reading news stories, studying photographs, and seeing how I might develop this material to create paintings of a sort in prose poetry. Here, then, are two series of prose poems that speak across the divides of time and place to the awful coincidences of youth and violence, in war and in peace.

Carrie Etter
Bath, England
June 2020

I. Toyen, 1939-40

The Shooting Gallery I

Toyen, 1939

So much birdseed scattered over the dry, cracked earth, and no birds. Well, no living birds: there's a painting of two pigeons' heads propped atop a pigeonhole cabinet (but no pigeons in the pigeonholes), a wooden decoy attached to a sapling, and a larger-than-life picture of a bird, painted onto glass only to shatter. A funeral wreath on a dead tree completes the makeshift memorial, but where are the mourners?

The Shooting Gallery II

Toyen, 1939

When I was eight or ten and wore dresses, to some adults I appeared a mere outline, girl-shape, faceless. This girl's puff sleeves make me think: Anne of Green Gables. Oh I remember child-size desires, glee come easy. Those beribboned, pointed shoes—and yet the slack in her jump-rope. Yes, in the field of broken glass, who would? The fool rooster eating the slivers as though they were kernels of corn—just look at him now, splayed on his back, feet in the air. No wonder the girl's face has disappeared.

The Shooting Gallery III

Toyen, 1939

For miles in every direction, broken eggshells, most shattered to small pieces. On one of the few still largely intact, the face of a little girl. The only bird left in the world perches on her cheek.

The Shooting Gallery IV

Toyen, 1939

A woman's face mid-scream: eyes squeezing shut, mouth
a darkly lipsticked oval. The face became a fairground
façade, ten feet high, and all those balls on the ground are for
hurling through the hole, into the howl. Those men in
overcoats had a go, pitching, laughing when one missed and
the plaster cracked at the blow. Yes, there are birdcages here
and there, but none has held a song.

The Shooting Gallery V

Toyen, 1939

Across the snowbound field, bird's nests, twigs interlaced to make a firm bowl, a bed, a place of rest. Twenty on the ground, one aloft in a dead sapling.

Where are the birds?

Among the nests stand two manmade birdhouses, each with two tall, arched openings, each decorated with miniature shuttered windows, a miniature stag's head.

Where are the birds?

There's no seeing inside the birdhouses or into the conical well of the sapling's nest.

At this stage, we cannot confirm the number of living or dead.

The Shooting Gallery VI

Toyen, 1939

Across the lawn, men have planted wooden birds—decoys—
to entice live ones hither. There's even one attached to the
shattered folding screen, to draw attention to the enormous
fishhead hanging from a hook. The fox's head holds another
fish: show the predator, and show his mouth already full.

The Shooting Gallery VII

Toyen, 1939

On the field, five missiles, about a meter high, stand here and there. This is an outdoor shooting gallery, and there are five targets, each painted on a board two meters tall. On one, a dog's open mouth, panting or barking. On another, a gagged woman, struggling to look away.

The Shooting Gallery VIII

Toyen, 1940

See the torsos of two young soldiers, arms roughly hacked off above the elbow, chests mounted on grooved walnut pedestals. On the boys' skin, the substance of their thoughts: school and its handwriting lessons; a circus girl lifting a barbell overhead, her short, tutu-like skirt revealing so much of her bare legs; a favourite pet; the good silver suggestive of a resplendent dinner with no quibble over seconds or even thirds.

Look at all those walnuts scattered on the plain, a windfall reminiscent of long summer days, bulging pockets, a son's bounty.

The Shooting Gallery IX

Toyen, 1940

The geese are shot and plucked, ready for roasting, but their theatre is crisscrossed by low-strung barbed wire. You will be sated, but first you will bleed.

The Shooting Gallery X

Toyen, 1940

Across the desolate plateau / battlefield / meadow, hundreds upon hundreds of funeral wreaths.

At the centre, you would take a seat, if you could only sit down, if there weren't a fox's head attached to the chair's back, a fox's head attached to the seat.

The fox chair says, Mourn the dead, but do not try to loiter, do not try to settle.

For the mourning, there is no rest.

The Shooting Gallery XI

Toyen, 1940

Scattered across the white plateau, feathers, feathers all the way to the horizon. Much too close the dismembered wing. The dead bird larger than the living, the ordinary. A few more steps to reach the bird's head, eyes open to what must be sky. Keep walking: another head. The skirted schoolgirl has turned her back, but she still casts a shadow.

The Shooting Gallery XII

Toyen, 1940

Is this the end of childhood? The castles constructed from building blocks look as though they've suffered an aerial bombardment, what with the missing roofs and broken towers. As for the rabbit emerging from a blasted fortress, once a girl named him. Once a girl, long gone, stroked his fur.

II. The United States, 1999-

The Shooting Gallery

Columbine High School, Colorado, 1999

Who knew that a teenage boy's brown pickup truck could sprout lilies, roses, carnations? And what about the balloons tied to the fender, sideview mirror, and tailgate? Inside the cab, over the bed, cellophane-wrapped bouquets rise amid cards, handwritten notes, a poem until all the empty space fills, until absence becomes presence, for a while.

The Shooting Gallery

Red Lion Junior High School, Pennsylvania, 2003

On the canvas's white field, cartoon thought-bubbles bob in the air. Each bubble shows a perfect red heart with a Bible before it, open to the Psalms. "Our hearts and prayers go out," the governor said at the televised press conference, and at home, viewers nodded, *hearts and prayers*.

Beneath the bubbles of Bibles and hearts lie the bodies of James Sheets and his principal, Eugene Segro. Their eyes are open, but they do not see the busy air.

The Shooting Gallery

Red Lake Senior High School, Minnesota, 2005

This canvas is not an empty tableau: it's an "Indian" reservation. In the air hang the victims' favourite things: a leather jacket, a teddy bear, a thinning velour blanket, a silver locket, a conch shell, and so on. Mothers and fathers wander the plain, some on their knees gathering sage for burning at the funerals, some looking up, a finger to their lips, as they try to decide what to place in the casket.

The Shooting Gallery

Virginia Tech, 2007

Lines of yellow police tape, too high to step over, too low to duck easily under, crisscross the green. Each segment of land has a single specimen: steel chains; a backpack spilling textbooks; a Glock 19; the corpse of a teenager.

Along the horizon, thirty-two candles burn.

The Shooting Gallery

Virginia Tech, 2007

On the far wall hang 32 clocks, each stopped between
seven-fifteen and nine fifty-two. In the foreground, Liviu
Lebrescu reclines in a black Eames lounge chair. In the afterlife,
people ask him not about his experience of the Holocaust
or about the university shooting, but about his work in
aeroplasticity and aerodynamics. He often pauses as he
answers, smiling broadly, and glances over his shoulder, where
out of the windows his students still climb.

The Shooting Gallery

University of Texas at Austin, 2010

Floating in the air as though ink could rise from a textbook are differential equations, a chaos of Xs and Ys, exponents and parentheses, equal and addition signs.

Prostrate below lies sophomore Colton Tooley, his face obscured by a ski mask, an AK-47 in a widening pool of blood next to his head.

The Shooting Gallery

Normal Community High School, Illinois, 2012

At first, what rattled / was the proximity, the intimacy— / gunfire only a mile from / my family home. For days I wore the knowledge / like chain mail, my torso / heavier, my shoulders / newly weighted. I Googled. I found in my town Darnall's Gun Works & Ranges, C.I. Shooting Sports. I found photos of / the aftermath, the brawny teacher leading a column of students / away, away, / the huddled parents, waiting, the / reunions, the mother and son— / — / the son's t-shirt: a drawing of a boy wearing his baseball cap backwards / his eye to the viewfinder / of a machine gun, its long belt of cartridges ready— / mother and son and his t-shirt—this / is where I come from.

The Shooting Gallery

Marysville Pilchuck High School, Washington, 2014

In the foreground, a round table from the cafeteria, surrounded by five empty chairs. At each place rests a teenager's phone showing a grinning selfie.

Not ten feet behind the table stands a leafless tree, dangling handguns.

The Shooting Gallery

Umpqua Community College, Oregon, 2015

President Obama stands at a podium bearing the presidential seal, his eyes closed—is he praying?

There's a long white table to either side of him. One bears all the paraphernalia of a college science classroom: beakers, a Bunsen burner, glass test tubes, a microscope. On the other table lie eighteen gun casings.

If you look closely, you can see Obama biting his lower lip.

The Shooting Gallery

Marjory Stoneman Douglas High School, Florida, 2018

White crosses, white Stars of David, each with a red heart, each with a name: Alyssa, Scott, Martin; Nicholas, Aaron, Jaime; Chris, Luke, Cara; Gina, Joaquin, Alaina; Meadow, Helena, Alex; Carmen and Peter. The litany of the dead includes eleven children. If I propose their names make a dirge, you will reply, *How very American.*

The Shooting Gallery

Santa Fe High School, Texas, 2018

In this art classroom, paintings and drawings cover an entire
wall: still lifes mingling fruit and ceramics; portraits surely
self-portraits given the apparent age of the faces; and life
drawings focusing on specific body parts—here a foot, there
a neck, and many hands sketched with attention to skin, veins,
knuckles.

At the back, in a large supply closet, teenagers hide as they hear
the shooter sing, "Another one bites the dust," as they hear his
footsteps just before the bullets.

The Shooting Gallery

Central Academy of Excellence, Missouri, 2019

There is snow on the ground, but in America, there is no such thing as a blank canvas. Wind drives a basketball across a parking lot, and Mylar balloons rise into a white sky: pink hearts amid blue, gold, and silver stars. In the place of an artist's signature in the lower right corner, a caption: Anjanique Wright, 15.

ABOUT THE AUTHOR

After nineteen years in Normal, Illinois, Carrie Etter moved to southern California, where she lived for the next thirteen years and ultimately pursued various degrees. She has lived in England since 2001 and is Reader in Creative Writing at Bath Spa University.

BY THE SAME AUTHOR

as author:
The Weather in Normal (UK: Seren; US: Station Hill, 2018)
Imagined Sons (Seren, 2014)
Divining for Starters (Shearsman, 2011)
The Tethers (Seren, 2009)

as editor:
Linda Lamus, *A Crater the Size of Calcutta* (Mulfran, 2015)
Infinite Difference: Other Poetries by UK Women Poets (Shearsman, 2010)

ACKNOWLEDGEMENTS

Some of the poems in this pamphlet first appeared in *The Fortnightly Review, Free Verse, Poetry Wales,* and *Tentacular.* I am grateful to Claire Crowther for her comments on the manuscript, Stuart Bartholomew for his unremitting interest and enthusiasm, and my London/National Theatre workshop group for feedback on a couple of the poems.

ABOUT VERVE POETRY PRESS

Verve Poetry Press is a quite new and already award-winning press that focussed initially on meeting a local need in Birmingham - a need for the vibrant poetry scene here in Brum to find a way to present itself to the poetry world via publication. Co-founded by Stuart Bartholomew and Amerah Saleh, it now publishes poets from all corners of the UK - poets that speak to the city's varied and energetic qualities and will contribute to its many poetic stories.

Added to this is a colourful pamphlet series, many featuring poets who have performed at our sister festival - and a poetry show series which captures the magic of longer poetry performance pieces by festival alumni such as Polarbear, Matt Abbott and Geraldine Carver.

Like the festival, we strive to think about poetry in inclusive ways and embrace the multiplicity of approaches towards this glorious art.

In 2019 the press was voted Most Innovative Publisher at the Saboteur Awards, and won the Publisher's Award for Poetry Pamphlets at the Michael Marks Awards.

www.vervepoetrypress.com
@VervePoetryPres
mail@vervepoetrypress.com